the PARABLES of JESUS

COLORING BOOK DEVOTIONAL

LAURA JAMES
and
KATARA WASHINGTON PATTON

Faith Words

New York Boston Nashville

FaithWords
Hachette Book Group
1290 Avenue of the Americas, New York, NY 10104
faithwords.com
twitter.com/faithwords

First Edition: January 2017

FaithWords is a division of Hachette Book Group, Inc. The FaithWords name and logo are trademarks of Hachette Book Group, Inc.

The publisher is not responsible for websites (or their content) that are not owned by the publisher.

The Hachette Speakers Bureau provides a wide range of authors for speaking events. To find out more, go to www.hachettespeakersbureau.com or call (866) 376-6591.

ISBN: 978-1-4555-9642-3 (trade pbk.)

Printed in the United States of America

Walsworth

10 9 8 7 6 5 4 3 2

To Kayla: I pray you learn to love God and God's Word through every season of your life. —KWP

For Manman. —LJ

Acknowledgments

Special thanks and appreciation to the Hachette team for including me on such an awesome project. Jesus told great stories, and I'm honored to retell them. —KWP

With love to Mennen, Zuri, and Neville, the stars in my universe. —LJ

Out with the Old, in with the New

Besides, who would patch old clothing with new cloth? For the new patch would shrink and rip away from the old cloth, leaving an even bigger tear than before.

Mark 2:21 NLT (also found in Matt. 9:16 and Luke 5:36)

As Jesus walked the earth teaching of the new way of life he was establishing, some people were confused. Some refused to give up old traditions and customs to follow the Savior. They may have been comfortable with the old religion, or they may not have quite trusted the new guy on the scene—with his vivid stories, miracles, healings, and profound teachings.

But Jesus preached that some things needed to be done away with. Not all old and new things mix well. And Jesus was the new. He was the Way. Jesus was the ultimate sacrifice, suffering our sins so that we could be saved. Out with the old and in with the new.

To illustrate that the new must be embraced, Jesus asked a question: If one wanted to repair an old piece of cloth, would they use a new piece of cloth to fix the old, worn garment? The seamstresses of the day would have known the answer—of course not! If an unshrunk (new) piece of cloth is sewn to a worn and shrunk one, it'd only create more trouble. The new cloth would not match and it would still have room to shrink when washed or worn. It would rip away from the cloth and create a bigger mess than before the repair. Only an equally worn patch should be used to fix an old garment.

Likewise, if you want to repair something new, you use a new piece of cloth—giving it the opportunity to change, stretch, or shrink at the same rate. And so it was with Jesus. Some of the old traditions needed to be done away with. Jesus was bringing in the new, salvation through acceptance of him and his sacrifice. You couldn't mix the old with the new. You either believed and accepted him, or you didn't.

Have you been mixing the old and the new? Old traditions you may have had before fully committing to Jesus or old habits you may be trying to fit into a new lifestyle? Use this parable to remind you to embrace the new and liberating lifestyle Jesus offers.

Is there an old habit you need to rid yourself of? Embrace the new today.

New Storage

And no one puts new wine into old wineskins. For the new wine would burst the wineskins, spilling the wine and ruining the skins. New wine must be stored in new wineskins.

Luke 5:37–38 NLT (also found in Matt. 9:17 and Mark 2:22)

For those who couldn't quite understand the concept of repairing new garments with new patches and old with old, Jesus told another story to illustrate his meaning. He used wine and wineskins to make the same point.

Goatskins were used to hold wine. Because wine is made of grapes, the wine changes, or ferments, as it gets older. The fermentation stretches the wineskins. Now, if you put new wine that has not yet fermented into an old wineskin, you're going to have trouble once the new wine ferments. The old skin will not be able to make room for the expanding wine, because the old skin has already been stretched to capacity. You'll end up with spilled wine, bursting out of the old wineskin. What a waste.

So, just like you need to use new patches to repair new garments, you need to put new wine in new skins. Keep the old in the old.

The Christian lifestyle should be reflective of this parable, too. There are some things you did when you didn't know Christ or didn't know any better. You may have tried to follow a set of ethics of your own design, which didn't exclude you from gossiping, fretting, scheming to get ahead—oh, the list may go on and on. But now that you have been introduced to a new life in Christ, you can forgo your old ways. You must allow God's spirit to fill you and lead you, not your own way. Along with this change comes a beautiful peace about life that only God provides. Every aspect of a new life in him is better. You can turn gossiping words into praises and worrying into prayers. Don't get stuck pouring old wine into new skins. Make room for the new, really good stuff.

Almighty Lord: Thank you for giving me a new life in Christ. Rid me of my old ways and my old way of thinking. Renew in me a clean, serene heart and mind to follow and serve you with each day. I lean and depend on you for all things, and I humbly follow Jesus' teachings for all things in my life.

Shine On!

You are the light of the world. A city that is set on a hill cannot be hidden. Nor do they light a lamp and put it under a basket, but on a lampstand, and it gives light to all who are in the house.

Matt. 5:14–15 NKJV

Have you ever wondered what your job is as a Christian? Jesus makes it clear through this parable. Each and every person who believes in Christ has a job—and that's to be an example, a light to the dark world. We are continually and constantly called to shine our lights brightly so others can see Christ. We should be examples of the unconditional love of Christ and the beautiful grace and mercy he dispenses to each of us daily.

As lights, we are not to hide or be silent; we are to stand up and show Christ to the world. We were not created to be lights in a basket or in a hidden place. We were called to be on display for all to see, just like a light goes on top of a lampstand instead of in a basket.

You've got an important job. How well are you shining? Are you connected to the source of your light to make sure you don't run out of power, which would cause your light to be dimmed? Are you sitting high upon the lampstand, where everyone can see and feel your glow? You've been called for just this, so shine. Brightly.

Write about how you will shine brightly today.

A Solid Foundation

As for everyone who comes to me and hears my words and puts them into practice, I will show you what they are like. They are like a man building a house, who dug down deep and laid the foundation on rock. When a flood came, the torrent struck that house but could not shake it, because it was well built. But the one who hears my words and does not put them into practice is like a man who built a house on the ground without a foundation. The moment the torrent struck that house, it collapsed and its destruction was complete.

Luke 6:47–49 NIV (also found in Matt. 7:24–27)

I've never built a house before, but I can understand this story Jesus shared about two homebuilders. One man, the wise one, dug down deep before he started building his home. He used rock, a solid surface, for the foundation of the home, understanding that a structure as large as a house needed to sit on something solid and firm. So, when the storms came—as they are inclined to do—the floodwaters struck the house, but it did not move. It was built on a solid foundation.

However, another man skipped the process of digging deep and putting down solid rock; he just built his house without laying down a foundation. As soon as a storm came and the torrent struck, that house came tumbling down and was destroyed completely.

You may be like me, far from capable of or willing to build a house. But you can still relate this story to your faith. When you read God's word and pray, do you walk away changed, putting the lessons into practice? Or do you read and walk away unchanged?

Part of living in God's Kingdom means we put into practice all we learn about God and godly living. We walk by God's spirit, not by our own desires. We listen to promptings reminding us what is right rather than giving in to what we know is wrong. Life has its ups and downs. Storms come, and some are so strong that we feel as if they can wipe us out. But, if we have a solid foundation—and have applied God's word to our everyday lives—we can rest assured that we will survive. Our homes, our lives, will not be destroyed. We have a solid foundation. And that's some good news.

Build your house on a solid foundation.

Draw a picture of a home built on a solid foundation to remind you to apply what you read in God's Word to your everyday life.

A Big Debt

Jesus said, "There were two men. Both men owed money to the same banker. One man owed him 500 silver coins. The other man owed him 50 silver coins. The men had no money, so they could not pay their debt. But the banker told the men that they did not have to pay him. Which one of those two men will love him more?"

Simon answered, "I think it would be the one who owed him the most money."

Jesus said to him, "You are right."

Luke 7:41–43 ERV

Sometimes we look at sins in degrees—some seem far worse than others. Or, we may think some people sin more than others. But Jesus presents another way to look at sin.

When addressing the sin issue, Jesus tells a story about two men who had debt. One owed the bank five hundred coins while another owed only fifty coins. When neither man could pay his debt, the banker canceled both of their debts. He wiped their slates clean. Neither one owed a cent.

And Jesus poses a question to his audience after sharing this story: Who do you think loves the banker more? Simon Peter answers just as we would: he says the man who had the most debt to be forgiven is the one who probably loves the banker most.

What a refreshing look at sin, especially when we stand with sin-blotted clothing, guilty of more than we'd like to share. There's good news: Jesus forgives! And when we understand and embrace his forgiving grace, we love him more and more.

So if you have a lot of sin to be forgiven, rejoice—you also have a lot of love to give. And think about all the love the sinners around you have to give, too. Let's remind them that they, too, can be forgiven.

Think about how much you have been forgiven and the hope for a joyful future. You don't have to be burdened by past mistakes and linger. Jesus forgives. How does your love of Christ compare to the sin he will cancel for you?

Be Humble

When Jesus noticed that all who had come to the dinner were trying to sit in the seats of honor near the head of the table, he gave them this advice: "When you are invited to a wedding feast, don't sit in the seat of honor. What if someone who is more distinguished than you has also been invited? The host will come and say, 'Give this person your seat.' Then you will be embarrassed, and you will have to take whatever seat is left at the foot of the table!

"Instead, take the lowest place at the foot of the table. Then when your host sees you, he will come and say, 'Friend, we have a better place for you!' Then you will be honored in front of all the other guests. For those who exalt themselves will be humbled, and those who humble themselves will be exalted."

Luke 14:7–11 NLT

Jesus is the guest of honor—wouldn't you want to sit next to him? Apparently all the people who heard this parable did, too. They were all trying to sit near the head of the table, near the guest of honor. They wanted the best seat in the house. Wouldn't you?

Again, Jesus presents a paradigm shift to worldly thinking. Jesus reminds his listeners that they shouldn't automatically run to the front of the line or the head of the table, expecting the best seat, the best position, the highest benefit, or the most of everything. That type of behavior is spawned from a lack of humility and an overdeveloped sense of self-importance. That attitude prevents us from fully acknowledging God's ultimate greatness. And it also sets us up for an embarrassing fall.

No, there's a more excellent way, says Jesus. He reminds us to be humble, to not assume we are great, the most deserving, or the big shot. We should take a seat in the back, and if the host wants to exalt us, the host will ask us to come up front. If God calls us forward, we will rise.

Living for Jesus equals living humbly. Those who live faithfully will be exalted in due time, but exaltation should not be our goal. When we think about the great sacrifice of Christ just for us, we should be glad to even be invited to the party. Any seat will do, we humbly say—and honestly mean.

It's an honor just to be in Jesus' presence, regardless of what seat we have. Practice humility. It looks a lot like Jesus.

In what areas of your life can you use more humility? Who can you put before you in order to imitate Jesus?

Where Is Your Treasure Stored?

Then he told them a story: "A rich man had a fertile farm that produced fine crops. He said to himself, 'What should I do? I don't have room for all my crops.' Then he said, 'I know! I'll tear down my barns and build bigger ones. Then I'll have room enough to store all my wheat and other goods. And I'll sit back and say to myself, "My friend, you have enough stored away for years to come. Now take it easy! Eat, drink, and be merry!"'

"But God said to him, 'You fool! You will die this very night. Then who will get everything you worked for?'

"Yes, a person is a fool to store up earthly wealth but not have a rich relationship with God."

Luke 12:16–21 NLT

While we can't buy our way into the Kingdom of God, there are things that can block us from entering into this Kingdom. There are just some things that don't fit into the Kingdom where Jesus reigns, where good trumps evil and we live according to God's way. Greed and selfish concerns cannot exist in the Kingdom of God. It's the antithesis of the Kingdom. It looks nothing like Jesus, who became the ultimate sacrifice for our sins.

When we are greedy, with a laser focus on ourselves, we can never have *enough*, like the man in the story. He had so much, but he wanted more. Instead of sharing his bounty as it grew even greater, his motivation was to find a way to keep it all.

But, given the somber fate that was to befall him that very night, how was he to benefit? He would not be alive to enjoy the worldly gain he hoarded all for himself. In the end, his wealth meant nothing.

I don't think Jesus wants us to be unwise stewards of our earnings. But I think Jesus wanted us to beware of greed, of thinking only of ourselves, of always wanting more without tending to need where we see it. That's not like Jesus. That's not like the Kingdom of God. And when our focus is on our relationship with God, we are rich. We realize we have the greatest gift of all, so we can share with others and be content with what we have and what we don't have.

How valuable is your relationship with God? How much do you invest in it?

Be Awake

Keep your shirts on; keep the lights on! Be like house servants waiting for their master to come back from his honeymoon, awake and ready to open the door when he arrives and knocks. Lucky the servants whom the master finds on watch! He'll put on an apron, sit them at the table, and serve them a meal, sharing his wedding feast with them. It doesn't matter what time of the night he arrives; they're awake—and so blessed!

You know that if the house owner had known what night the burglar was coming, he wouldn't have stayed out late and left the place unlocked. So don't you be slovenly and careless. Just when you don't expect him, the Son of Man will show up.

Luke 12:35–40 MSG

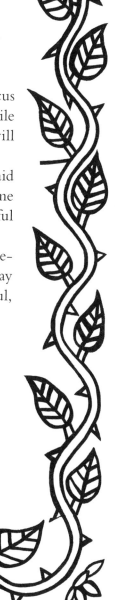

Living this life as a Christian can feel tedious at times—trying to love, trying to do right, and keeping our focus on God and all he wants us to do. Yes, it can wear on us at times and make us wonder if it's all worth it. While deep down we know it is, we can grow weary waiting on the full manifestation of God's Kingdom, when all will be set right.

Jesus knew that and told a story to encourage believers to keep waiting and watching and to stay alert. Jesus said we should always be awake, expecting our master to come home. We don't know the exact itinerary or the time he will be home, but if he returns and finds us awake and ready for him, he's going to share something wonderful with us.

Naturally, if we knew what time Jesus would return, we'd set our clocks and be ready, much like the homeowner would be at home and prepared if he knew what time a thief was going to show up. We don't know the day or the time, but we do know he will return, so we need to stay ready. We need to stay awake, alert, and hopeful, waiting on our true master to return.

When you are tempted to grow weary, remember to stay alert and await God. Draw a picture to remind you to stay awake.

Stay Ready

The Lord answered, "Who then is the faithful and wise manager, whom the master puts in charge of his servants to give them their food allowance at the proper time? It will be good for that servant whom the master finds doing so when he returns. Truly I tell you, he will put him in charge of all his possessions. But suppose the servant says to himself, 'My master is taking a long time in coming,' and he then begins to beat the other servants, both men and women, and to eat and drink and get drunk. The master of that servant will come on a day when he does not expect him and at an hour he is not aware of. He will cut him to pieces and assign him a place with the unbelievers.

"The servant who knows the master's will and does not get ready or does not do what the master wants will be beaten with many blows. But the one who does not know and does things deserving punishment will be beaten with few blows. From everyone who has been given much, much will be demanded; and from the one who has been entrusted with much, much more will be asked."

Luke 12:42–48 NIV (also found in Matt. 24:45–51)

Jesus must have known we'd have some trouble waiting, so he shared several stories to help us get ready as we await his coming, including this parable. Those of us who've been called to manage God's affairs while we await the Second Coming have a high calling. We know God's Word. We know God's plans. We know God's promises. We've been blessed with an amazing gift, and God expects to return finding us handling these gifts wisely. When he does, we will be rewarded and will be able to live in the Kingdom.

But if upon Christ's return we are found lazy in our faith, slacking, not alert to the needs of those around us, unprepared to enter the Kingdom, and not living according to God's plan, like the second manager in the parable, we, too, will be cast out like unbelievers. What a shame to make it so far but not really make it. That's not what we're living for! That's not our destiny. Live today like you want to receive the reward from God. Be faithful to the end.

Draw a picture of you crossing the finish line. What do you need to do to keep going and stay focused on your goal?

Bear Fruit

Then he told this parable: "A man had a fig tree growing in his vineyard, and he went to look for fruit on it but did not find any. So he said to the man who took care of the vineyard, 'For three years now I've been coming to look for fruit on this fig tree and haven't found any. Cut it down! Why should it use up the soil?'

"'Sir,' the man replied, 'leave it alone for one more year, and I'll dig around it and fertilize it. If it bears fruit next year, fine! If not, then cut it down.'"

Luke 13:6–9 NIV

As Christians, we should bear fruit, and our fruit should look, taste, and smell like Jesus. If we are not bearing fruit in line with Jesus' model, we need to change—right now. Consider this parable.

A man grew a tree, and not just so it would decorate his vineyard. He grew a tree for the purposes of it bearing fruit. He was expecting to see fruit on the tree he grew. So the man had a frank talk with the caretaker of the vineyard. The owner of the vineyard told the caretaker to cut the tree down; after all, he had been coming to see the vineyard for three years and had not yet seen fruit on the fig tree. That tree was taking up valuable space and using good soil, but it was not producing fruit. It was not living out its purpose.

But the caretaker intervened and asked for a little reprieve, time to add fertilizer to see if the tree would bear fruit. However, if the tree didn't yield any fruit and start fulfilling its destiny after a year, the caretaker would go ahead and cut it down.

What a message! We, too, are called to live our intended purpose—to yield fruit—and point others to the love of Christ. Thankfully, our master has also given us a reprieve, a chance to live and improve when we haven't approached life as we're supposed to. Let this parable be a reminder to us to make sure we live the life we're called to live as God's messengers to the world.

Review the fruits of the spirit found in Galatians 5:22—love, joy, peace, patience, kindness, goodness, and faithfulness. Which fruit do you need to bear more of? Pray for God's help.

Good Ground

"As he scattered it across his field, some of the seed fell on a footpath, and the birds came and ate it. Other seed fell on shallow soil with underlying rock. The seed sprouted quickly because the soil was shallow. But the plant soon wilted under the hot sun, and since it didn't have deep roots, it died. Other seed fell among thorns that grew up and choked out the tender plants so they produced no grain. Still other seeds fell on fertile soil, and they sprouted, grew, and produced a crop that was thirty, sixty, and even a hundred times as much as had been planted!" Then he said, "Anyone with ears to hear should listen and understand." [...]

Then Jesus said to them, "If you can't understand the meaning of this parable, how will you understand all the other parables? The farmer plants seed by taking God's word to others. The seed that fell on the footpath represents those who hear the message, only to have Satan come at once and take it away. The seed on the rocky soil represents those who hear the message and immediately receive it with joy. But since they don't have deep roots, they don't last long. They fall away as soon as they have problems or are persecuted for believing God's word. The seed that fell among the thorns represents others who hear God's word, but all too quickly the message is crowded out by the worries of this life, the lure of wealth, and the desire for other things, so no fruit is produced. And the seed that fell on good soil represents those who hear and accept God's word and produce a harvest of thirty, sixty, or even a hundred times as much as had been planted!"

Mark 4:4–9, 13–20 NLT (full parable can be found in Mark 4:3–20;
also found in Matt. 13:3–23 and Luke 8:4–15)

In this parable the seed is the Word of God, the pathway God has given us to follow. The first seed, which Satan steals, is truth that cannot take root because the hearts of those who it's meant for are too overcome with darkness to receive it. The seed that falls on a rocky path represents the Word falling upon zealous people who receive it with joy and are impacted by the promise of its life-changing power. However, because these people don't have a solid foundation of dedication and the discipline to practice their faith, they soon lose the hope, joy, and commitment to live out the Word. And then the seed caught up by the thorns represents those who allow the worry and cares of this world to cancel out what they have heard. The Word can't form and grow within them because their focus is elsewhere. But the ones we should strive to emulate are like the seed that falls on good ground—ground that is primed, watered, fertilized, and ready to receive all that the Word exposes and expresses. This person allows the seed to take root on a solid foundation and helps it to grow, flourish, and multiply, which ultimately blesses others. This is our God-given purpose.

Oh, to be a seed that flourishes.

Draw a picture of yourself as a seed, responding to the Word of God. How do you want to grow?

When Weeds Grow . . .

He told them another parable, saying, "The kingdom of heaven is like a man who sowed good seed in his field. But while men slept, his enemy came and sowed weeds among the wheat and went away. But when the shoots had sprung up and produced fruit, the weeds also appeared. [. . .]

"Let both grow together until the harvest, and in the time of harvest I will say to the reapers: 'Gather up the weeds first and bind them in bundles to burn them, but gather the wheat into my barn.'" [. . .]

He answered, "He who sows the good seed is the Son of Man, the field is the world, and the good seed are the sons of the kingdom. But the weeds are the sons of the evil one. The enemy who sowed them is the devil, the harvest is the end of the world, and the reapers are the angels."

Matt. 13:24–26, 30, 37–39 MEV **(full parable found in Matt. 13:24–30, 36–43)**

On this Christian journey, we will no doubt encounter people who don't seem genuine. Sure, they may say they are Christians, but through our experiences with them we sense that something isn't right.

Living among fake Christians is just like today's parable, in which a man plants good seed while his enemy tries to sabotage his efforts by planting weeds among the good seed. When weeds pop up, noticeably different than the wheat, some of the farmworkers want to pull the weeds right away—expose the false proclaimers immediately. But Jesus' story denounces that approach. If the weeds are pulled, the good wheat comes out with them. The faithful can be hurt in the messy process of sorting through those who are false.

The wise farmer knows the time will come to harvest the wheat and destroy the weeds. So he waits. Likewise, as Christians, we need to wait on Jesus to be the master sorter. He will separate the righteous from the evil.

Just make sure you're producing wheat and not weeds. God will handle the rest.

Gracious God, thank you for reminding me that you are the true farmer and harvest time is coming. Keep me on your path so that I may produce good fruit and not be a hindrance to anyone else. Remind me to focus on you and not those around me who may or may not be true. Amen.

A Faithful Planter

Then Jesus said, "God's kingdom is like seed thrown on a field by a man who then goes to bed and forgets about it. The seed sprouts and grows—he has no idea how it happens. The earth does it all without his help: first a green stem of grass, then a bud, then the ripened grain. When the grain is fully formed, he reaps—harvest time!"

Mark 4:26–29 MSG

Many of Jesus' parables were about farming. For an audience who understood agriculture, Jesus drew picture after picture to help them understand the life-changing gospel message. This parable shares a simple picture of how a seed grows. The planter who throws a seed on the ground may water it or make sure it's in good dirt, but he—the human—doesn't do much to make the seed grow. But the seed does grow. The earth does the work without the man's help.

The Kingdom of God is the same way. The Word of God can be sprinkled over our hearts; it can be spread through songs, sermons, and life examples. We just need to plant it and watch God do the work without any other help from us. We can go to bed and wait to see the crop sprout, bud, and eventually grow into a full harvest.

If there's someone in your life who needs salvation, make sure you've thrown a seed their way. Keep praying and watch the seed grow without any extra help from you.

We're called to be faithful planters, to wait, and to watch God do the rest.

Write a letter to plant a seed in someone's life today.

Small Beginnings

The Kingdom of Heaven is like a mustard seed planted in a field. It is the smallest of all seeds, but it becomes the largest of garden plants; it grows into a tree, and birds come and make nests in its branches.

Matt. 13:31–32 NLT (also found in Mark 4:30–32 and Luke 13:18–19)

Jesus' early followers may have been wondering just how the Kingdom of God (or Heaven) would come about when only a few followers had learned to trust and depend on the words of the carpenter from Galilee. Jesus was not going to let his believers wonder about this. He used another agriculture-related story to help them understand how the Kingdom of God would expand.

At the time of the story, the mustard seed was the smallest seed known to farmers. You could fit at least fifty mustard seeds on a modern-day penny. That's pretty small. But the mustard tree can grow up to ten feet tall. Originally no bigger than one-fiftieth of a penny, what a great height and size it can reach! Reflecting on the growth of that tiny seed into a large tree had to create a poignant image in the listeners' minds. Likewise, Jesus wanted them to understand just how large the Christian faith would expand.

Jesus began with twelve disciples and a few other followers, including those who had been healed and those who had witnessed. But consider his following now. People across the globe now call on the name of Jesus for salvation and follow God's Word for holy living.

In our lives, we don't have to worry about small beginnings. With God, the possibilities are limitless. From a tiny seed to an amazing Kingdom. That's enough to make me believe!

Draw a penny with small seeds inside of it. Then draw a tree that is far larger than the penny. Reflect on how your faith can grow and how God's Kingdom has grown.

A Little Yeast

Another story. "God's kingdom is like yeast that a woman works into the dough for dozens of loaves of barley bread—and waits while the dough rises."

Matt. 13:33 MSG (also found in Luke 13:20–21)

An equal-opportunity Jesus has a story that not only the farmers can relate to, but the bakers can as well. Whoever you are, Jesus wants to make this lesson resonate with you. What starts off small can expand into something larger than your wildest dreams.

Take, for example, a little bit of yeast. Most bread recipes call for a little bit of yeast (a teaspoon or so per loaf). But when that yeast is worked into the dough and put into the oven, it rises and produces a full loaf of bread. What starts off small expands. What begins flat rises up. What seems insignificant can become mouthwatering goodness.

Just a little bit can produce a lot.

Let's not worry about the numbers, whether in our faith community or in the number of hours we have to dedicate. Jesus has shown us time and time again that it just takes a little bit. The Kingdom of God can expand from almost nothing into something large and amazing. And like yeast, we may not understand how it works—we just know it works. Add just a little bit of faith to your efforts and watch them grow really big.

Creator God, increase my faith to the size of a teaspoon of yeast so that I may watch you work within me and produce enough bread to feed others. A little yeast equals a lot of bread. A little faith equals great things. I believe.

A Treasure

God's kingdom is like a treasure hidden in a field for years and then accidentally found by a trespasser. The finder is ecstatic—what a find!—and proceeds to sell everything he owns to raise money and buy that field.

Matt. 13:44 MSG

The Kingdom of God—where wrong is made right and the world submits to the true King—is available to every believer. What a gift we have been offered, a great feast in which we've been invited to freely partake.

In this parable, Jesus says that finding the Kingdom of God is like finding a hidden treasure—a jewel, gold, or millions upon millions of dollars. If you found such a treasure, you might be inclined to do like the trespasser. He knows that the treasure is of such great value, he should buy the field where it lay and, as a result, make the treasure his. He sells everything to gain the field. It's worth every penny he has; it's worth his current lifestyle; it's worth his being called crazy and a lunatic. He knows what he's getting when he buys this field, and he's willing to do whatever needs to be done to get the treasure.

Oh, that we could be like the trespasser and realize what great treasure we have, one worth the sacrifice of all we have. But the treasure we have has no monetary price. It's free and we've already been invited to take it. But although it's freely given, that doesn't mean its value should be taken for granted. Being in the Kingdom of God should outrank any of our goals, desires, or possessions. Thus, we must lose ourselves to the world to be found in him and accept the treasure. This treasure should be at the top of our minds and at the root of our hearts' desires.

Are you treating God's invitation to the Kingdom too lightly? Have you forgotten the precious value of this treasure? What must you do today to acknowledge the value of God's treasure above all else?

Heavenly God, I need to remember that the gift of your Kingdom is so very precious. It's the best treasure I could ever desire. Forgive me for taking the gift for granted. I desire to honor the gift and the Gift Giver by living according to your will each and every day. Amen.

A Fine Pearl

Again, the kingdom of heaven is like a merchant looking for fine pearls. When he found one of great value, he went away and sold everything he had and bought it.

Matt. 13:45–46 NIV

Some things are worth repeating. Understanding the value of the Kingdom of God (also called the Kingdom of Heaven) is apparently of great significance to Jesus' followers. Jesus repeats this lesson by comparing the Kingdom of God to a valuable pearl.

Pearls are considered precious gems even today. They are valued. They are delicate. They are beautiful. And in this parable a merchant is looking for fine pearls, the best of the best. So, when he finds one, he acts quickly. He does everything he needs to do to secure this rare beauty. The merchant evidently knows a good thing when he sees it. And he, like the trespasser in the parable of the hidden treasure, gives all he has to purchase this pearl of great value.

Remember, the Kingdom of God is not for sale, but it is even more valuable than the rarest gem or biggest treasure. Within the Kingdom of God life is as it should be, in line with God and God's values. We lose our selfishness; we are more loving and more merciful. The Kingdom ministers justice with grace and compassion, stands up for the oppressed, and advocates for the least of these. The Kingdom of God is some treasure, and we can belong. But are we willing to sacrifice to secure our place?

"Whoever wants to be my disciple must deny themselves and take up their cross daily and follow me" (Luke 9:23 NIV). We need to pursue God's Kingdom with as much vigor as the merchant pursues the pearl. Have you taken up your cross today?

———

Pursue the Kingdom. What are some of the things you need to rid yourself of to better enjoy the Kingdom of God today?

The Good and the Bad

Or, God's kingdom is like a fishnet cast into the sea, catching all kinds of fish. When it is full, it is hauled onto the beach. The good fish are picked out and put in a tub; those unfit to eat are thrown away. That's how it will be when the curtain comes down on history. The angels will come and cull the bad fish and throw them in the garbage. There will be a lot of desperate complaining, but it won't do any good.

Matt. 13:47–50 MSG

Jesus often illustrated the same point in several different ways. It must have been very important to him for us to understand, and so he served up the message in different ways to help us out. Simply put, Jesus wanted us to know that we don't have to worry about evildoers, pretenders, perpetrators, haters, and so on. They will all be dealt with in due time.

In this parable, Jesus uses a fishing analogy to make his point. Fishing was a common occupation at the time, and he compares the Kingdom of God to a fisherman casting his net into the sea. When he pulls that net up, there are a variety of fish in it. He isn't concerned with what type he has caught just yet. But when he is ready to haul the fish, he takes them to the shore. He then goes through the fish, keeping the good catch in a tub and throwing away the fish that aren't suitable to eat.

So don't fret or worry when you seem to be caught up in the same net as some bad fish. You will only be in their company for a little while. Eventually our Master Fisherman will do some separating and will preserve all of those who are following the Way. Then, like the chosen fish, we won't be among the bad any longer.

Ask God for help today to show patience, love, and kindness to all of those around you, even when it's difficult. Remember that he will take care of you, and judgment and vengeance are not yours. Let God sort the fish, and by following his example of love you are sure to remain in his favor.

The New and the Old

He said, "Then you see how every student well-trained in God's kingdom is like the owner of a general store who can put his hands on anything you need, old or new, exactly when you need it."

Matt. 13:52 MSG

When Jesus came, he came to fulfill the law of the Old Testament. While he didn't want his followers to forget about the old or do away with it, he did need them to understand the depth of what he was doing: instituting a new covenant with us, a new agreement that fulfilled all of God's promises to us.

The new covenant, created and sealed with Jesus' death and resurrection, means we can openly and joyfully enter into a loving relationship with God. We don't have to check off a list of dos and don'ts. We don't have to sacrifice a certain animal during a certain time of year. We don't risk getting stoned for an offense or sin. We can openly enjoy our relationship with God when we accept that Jesus paid the ultimate sacrifice for our sins.

I like to say that recognizing what God has done for us through Christ makes us want to follow the laws, rules, and regulations set into place in the Old Testament—after all, they were written for the people's good and to help them stay on course. However, we don't have to be bound to the law and worried about each rule and regulation because we have accepted the sacrifice of Christ. There's freedom in knowing Christ. There's freedom in this relationship and this new covenant (Galatians 5:1).

Jesus' parable shows how the old and the new should work together. Jesus says that a good store owner knows where the old and the new are. He's well aware of all he has in his store. And as Christians, while we may not follow all the rules and regulations of the old covenant, we are still good store owners and we know where things are. We are fully aware of the freedom of the new covenant and we understand the principles of the old covenant. They were both put in place to help us, and because we love God, we want to follow God's way.

It's freeing to live under the new covenant, and it makes us want to do right.

Which commandments or laws from the Old Testament do you follow today? How do they help you live according to God's will?

One Lost Sheep

Look at it this way. If someone has a hundred sheep and one of them wanders off, doesn't he leave the ninety-nine and go after the one? And if he finds it, doesn't he make far more over it than over the ninety-nine who stay put? Your Father in heaven feels the same way. He doesn't want to lose even one of these simple believers.

Matt. 18:12–14 MSG

Jesus calls himself the good shepherd (John 10:14). He proclaims himself to be the guide and leader who tenderly cares for all of us committed to following him. As any good shepherd does, he keeps his steady gaze on each of us, to protect us and keep us safe from attacks. He makes sure we are well taken care of and can enjoy the pastures. But when one strays, when one wanders from his protective gaze as wayward sheep can do, he searches for us. Our shepherd looks high and low for the one who is lost, even leaving the other sheep.

Now our Omnipresent Lord doesn't need to leave his position to spot a wayward believer, but this parable illustrates his sincere concern for each of us. Just as a shepherd would leave ninety-nine sheep in a pasture to look for just one lost sheep, Jesus yearns for the lost believer to return to the safety of the pasture, the safety found in fellowship with Christ. In his sight, each lost sheep or lost believer is just as precious as all of the rest.

Thank you, Lord! I rejoice because you love and care for me so genuinely. I never want to leave your fold, but if I do, I am thankful for your loving invitation to return.

The Ultimate Shepherd

I am the good shepherd. The good shepherd sacrifices his life for the sheep. A hired hand will run when he sees a wolf coming. He will abandon the sheep because they don't belong to him and he isn't their shepherd. And so the wolf attacks them and scatters the flock. The hired hand runs away because he's working only for the money and doesn't really care about the sheep.

I am the good shepherd; I know my own sheep, and they know me just as my Father knows me and I know the Father. So I sacrifice my life for the sheep. I have other sheep, too, that are not in this sheepfold. I must bring them also. They will listen to my voice, and there will be one flock with one shepherd.

The Father loves me because I sacrifice my life so I may take it back again. No one can take my life from me. I sacrifice it voluntarily. For I have the authority to lay it down when I want to and also to take it up again. For this is what my Father has commanded.

John 10:11–18 NLT (full parable found in John 10:1–5, 7–18)

Listen to the words of Jesus. He is your shepherd, but not only your shepherd—he is also the good shepherd. He does his job well. He gently cares for each and every one of his sheep. How much does he care? He cares enough to sacrifice his own life for yours. He's the ultimate shepherd, not the hired hand who runs when under attack. No, the ultimate shepherd protects at all costs. He even protected us from sin by giving his own life, the ultimate sacrifice. He is the ultimate protector, the ultimate shepherd.

Oh, what joy we can have because we are led and guided by the ultimate shepherd who gave the ultimate sacrifice. He did it voluntarily, because he had the power to give up his life as well as gain new life. Oh, what joy we have because we are protected by the ultimate shepherd. We have only to follow his loving directions.

Write how it feels to be saved and led by the ultimate shepherd, Jesus Christ.

Do Your Job

When a servant comes in from plowing or taking care of sheep, does his master say, "Come in and eat with me"? No, he says, "Prepare my meal, put on your apron, and serve me while I eat. Then you can eat later." And does the master thank the servant for doing what he was told to do? Of course not. In the same way, when you obey me you should say, "We are unworthy servants who have simply done our duty."

Luke 17:7–10 NLT

In a world full of entitled attitudes, this parable hits home. It is another Jesus shared about a servant and his master. He posed a scenario for us, his followers, to ponder.

If the servant came in from doing some hard work outside, such as plowing the fields or shepherding the sheep, would the master ask the servant to sit down and eat or would the master give the servant further instructions, such as what to prepare for dinner?

The answer is pretty obvious: of course the master wouldn't invite the servant to sit down and eat. The servant is at work and is expected to do just that—work. I'm sure Jesus is not advocating abusive labor practices or condoning the practices of chattel slavery, but Jesus is saying a servant should expect to serve his master.

And likewise, Jesus' followers shouldn't expect special treatment or accolades for doing what we're supposed to do—live a life that reflects the true nature and calling of Jesus. I know it's easy to look around and see others getting pats on the back, which can make us wonder where our applause is. We've been groomed to expect to hear "Job well done." It's a part of our nature and culture. But, according to Jesus, we shouldn't expect this type of treatment. Humility should kick in. We should recognize that it's our job to show Christ to others, to exemplify Christ. It's what we're called to do, so let's get to it.

Master and Almighty Lord, forgive me for feeling entitled to receive praise and recognition for living as your disciple. I am your servant, called to show your grace, mercy, love, and way to this world. When I want to be applauded, remind me that I am doing the job I am supposed to do. Help me to seek your approval and your approval only. Compared to your grace, I know I am an unworthy servant and am grateful to be in service to you. Amen.

Forgive

Then the master called the servant in. "You wicked servant," he said, "I canceled all that debt of yours because you begged me to. Shouldn't you have had mercy on your fellow servant just as I had on you?" In anger his master handed him over to the jailers to be tortured, until he should pay back all he owed.

This is how my heavenly Father will treat each of you unless you forgive your brother or sister from your heart.

Matt. 18:32–35 NIV (full parable found in Matt. 18:21–35)

Forgiveness is hard—especially when a loved one wounds you. We can retreat, vowing never to love again. We can respond to being hurt by inflicting pain on anyone else around us. After all, hurting people hurt people. We can stuff our feelings deep down, hoping they never erupt and showcase our full range of pain, all the while causing internal harm to ourselves. None of these options will ever bring true joy, and we know it. But they do feel like safer choices, choices that guard us from more pain.

There is another option, and yes, it is forgiveness. But how? It hurts, really bad.

When I once had to deal with a painful experience, I stumbled across the parable of the unmerciful servant. I knew the story. It was often taught in Sunday school: be nice to others, render mercy, and don't be like the unmerciful servant who receives mercy but denies it to another man who owes him. But it wasn't until I read verse 35 and connected it with the rest of the parable that I stopped in my grudge-holding tracks: "This is how my heavenly Father will treat each of you unless you forgive your brother or sister from your heart."

Yikes! If I don't forgive my brother or sister, God will not forgive me? I need God's forgiveness, every single day. So I need to figure out a way to forgive my brother and my sister, quickly. When we compare the debt we owe God to the debt others owe us, we come up short every time.

I know it's hard. I know your brother or sister hurt you. But instead of focusing on their actions, try focusing on God's actions. His grace and mercy are new each day (Lamentations 3:22–23). I don't want to be in a position where I'm thanking God for forgiving my big debt and I can't cancel a much smaller debt for my sister or brother. That's just not right. So when I find myself needing to forgive someone, I beseech God for help. I wait for him to help me release pain and anger, and to provide me with wisdom to handle the person or situation that hurt me. I can't carry the debt of my sins, so I have to let others' debts go. I need the forgiveness of God to flow throughout my life.

Let it go! What's keeping you from forgiving someone? Draw a picture symbolizing you releasing the situation to God.

A Good Neighbor

Jesus answered by telling a story. "There was once a man traveling from Jerusalem to Jericho. On the way he was attacked by robbers. They took his clothes, beat him up, and went off leaving him half-dead. Luckily, a priest was on his way down the same road, but when he saw him he angled across to the other side. Then a Levite religious man showed up; he also avoided the injured man.

"A Samaritan traveling the road came on him. When he saw the man's condition, his heart went out to him. He gave him first aid, disinfecting and bandaging his wounds. Then he lifted him onto his donkey, led him to an inn, and made him comfortable. In the morning he took out two silver coins and gave them to the innkeeper, saying, 'Take good care of him. If it costs any more, put it on my bill—I'll pay you on my way back.'

"What do you think? Which of the three became a neighbor to the man attacked by robbers?"

"The one who treated him kindly," the religion scholar responded.

Jesus said, "Go and do the same."

Luke 10:30–37 MSG

Jesus was a master storyteller, often answering questions with one of his parables, like he does in this passage. When a man asked Jesus to define *neighbor*, Jesus replied with the well-known story of the Good Samaritan. And the answer would have been eye-opening.

Of three people who see a robbed, beaten man while they're traveling the same road, only a Samaritan stops to help—not a priest and not a Levite, both of whom would have been revered for their religious status. Samaritans were not considered as holy as priests or Levites.

Jesus also has a question for his questioner. He asks the man who he thinks the neighbor is in the story. Of course, the man has to say the Samaritan—even though Samaritans were considered foreigners and enemies of the Jewish audience first hearing this story. Regardless, the Samaritan's actions were undeniably the most neighborly. Therefore, Jesus illustrates that showing care and being kind is what neighbors do. We are all to go and do likewise. No matter what, are all called and capable.

Who are you caring for today? How are you being neighborly?

Persistence Pays Off

Then Jesus said to them, "Suppose one of you went to your friend's house at midnight and said to him, 'Friend, loan me three loaves of bread. A friend of mine has come into town to visit me, but I have nothing for him to eat.' Your friend inside the house answers, 'Don't bother me! The door is already locked, and my children and I are in bed. I cannot get up and give you anything.' I tell you, if friendship is not enough to make him get up to give you the bread, your boldness will make him get up and give you whatever you need. So I tell you, ask, and God will give to you. Search, and you will find. Knock, and the door will open for you. Yes, everyone who asks will receive. The one who searches will find. And everyone who knocks will have the door opened. If your children ask for a fish, which of you would give them a snake instead? Or, if your children ask for an egg, would you give them a scorpion? Even though you are bad, you know how to give good things to your children. How much more your heavenly Father will give the Holy Spirit to those who ask him!"

Luke 11:5–13 NCV

Jesus wants us to understand the very special relationship we have with the Father because of Jesus' gift of salvation. We have a Father waiting to hear us, and we can approach him boldly. Because Jesus has made a way for us to approach God, we can and we should.

Jesus relates our relationship with God to an earthly friend. The friend, who is in bed and being asked for bread, is not very happy. It's late. He's trying to sleep and so is his family. He will not give the seeker bread just because they are friends. He will not get up out of his warm bed and search through his kitchen for the other man. It's too late for all of that.

However, the persistence of the seeker will make his friend throw off the covers and break his sleep. The seeker doesn't listen to the no. He doesn't listen to the refusal. He keeps asking. He needs this bread!

And likewise, if we who have a special relationship with God through Christ would keep asking for what we need, we will receive it. Not because we are friends, but because we are persistent. If we ask, we shall receive.

And to drive the point home, Jesus reminds us that even humans like us know how to give the right gift. And God is much greater than we are. So, imagine what God has in store for those of us who dare to go boldly to the throne and present our requests? God's got what we need. We just need to ask.

What do you need today? How persistent is your request to God? Take a moment of prayer and ask him for what you need.

Shine Brightly

He said to them, "A lamp is not brought in to be put under a basket or under a bed, is it? Is it not [brought in] to be put on the lampstand? For nothing is hidden, except to be revealed; nor has anything been kept secret, but that it would come to light [that is, things are hidden only temporarily, until the appropriate time comes for them to be known]."

Mark 4:21–22 AMP (also found in Matt. 5:14–16, Luke 8:16–17, and Luke 11:33–36)

Stories. Parables. Illustrations. What's the whole point to all of Jesus' rhetoric? Not just words, not just stories, but wisdom to live by. It's what gives us life. It's what gives us direction, hope, and wealth. Oh, yes, it's more than stories and words and great analogies.

And, as in this illustration, it all has a major purpose.

Much like a lamp that is meant to illuminate and shed light in darkness, we are to take our God-given knowledge and shed light in this dark world. We Christians are called to be lights. We are to embrace, reenact, and profess the goodness of God so others can see it and be drawn toward his light.

It's not a secret. There's no code. The good news is meant to be shared. God's light in us is meant to draw others near. The light is meant to be used in the dark to the benefit of others.

How are you living? Is your light shining bright, or is it hidden? Are others drawn toward your light? What can you do today to let your little light shine?

Excuses, Excuses, Excuses

Jesus replied with this story: "A man prepared a great feast and sent out many invitations. When the banquet was ready, he sent his servant to tell the guests, 'Come, the banquet is ready.' But they all began making excuses. One said, 'I have just bought a field and must inspect it. Please excuse me.' Another said, 'I have just bought five pairs of oxen, and I want to try them out. Please excuse me.' Another said, 'I just got married, so I can't come.'

"The servant returned and told his master what they had said. His master was furious and said, 'Go quickly into the streets and alleys of the town and invite the poor, the crippled, the blind, and the lame.'"

Luke 14:16–21 NLT (full parable found in Luke 14:16–24; also found in Matt. 22:2–14)

We've all been invited to a great banquet—the abundant life available in the Kingdom of God. But all have not accepted the generous invitation. Are you like one of the guests invited to the banquet? You are full of reasons why you just can't stop what you're doing to attend. Or have you asked to put the invitation on hold until you're older or more ready? Do you have something else you're tending to that has garnered more importance than God's loving invitation?

Think twice about making excuses not to fully embrace God's loving invitation and enter gratefully into the Kingdom at hand. We don't know the time or the day this invitation will expire. Or when your invitation will be revoked and your place symbolically given away, because you didn't accept the invitation in time. Stop the excuses and commit fully to Christ today, while the invitation is still extended.

If you haven't fully committed to following Jesus, list why. Pray and ask for help to fully accept the invitation today. The host is graciously waiting your attendance.

Count the Cost

Suppose one of you wants to build a tower. Won't you first sit down and estimate the cost to see if you have enough money to complete it? For if you lay the foundation and are not able to finish it, everyone who sees it will ridicule you, saying, "This person began to build and wasn't able to finish."

Or suppose a king is about to go to war against another king. Won't he first sit down and consider whether he is able with ten thousand men to oppose the one coming against him with twenty thousand? If he is not able, he will send a delegation while the other is still a long way off and will ask for terms of peace. In the same way, those of you who do not give up everything you have cannot be my disciples.

Luke 14:28–33 NIV (full parable found in Luke 14:25–35)

Salvation is free, a gift from Christ, but living the Christian life does require sacrifice. And sacrifice shouldn't be agreed to blindly or lightly. To highlight the importance of considering the cost before we sign up, Jesus tells two stories. One is about a builder. What would happen if a man started building a house and had not considered how much it would cost to complete the project? What sense would that make? If he wanted a completed house, he should have known how much it would cost and made sure he had enough money to finish the project. An incomplete house—one with just a foundation—is of no use to anyone.

To further illustrate the importance of full commitment to God, Jesus also tells a story about a warrior king who engaged in war before considering whether he could win or if a different course of action would be more appropriate.

If we are going to run this Christian race, we should first consider the cost. Are we willing to go to the end? Do we have what we need to finish the journey? If we look closely, we will see that God has provided all we need to make it. We, however, have to pack the resolve and determination to utilize the tools he's given us. Then we can finish the house and win the war. It's worth the cost.

Need some resolve to continue on your journey? Review the help God has given to you by reading Romans 8:31–39. After you've considered the cost (and benefits), journal about your decision to keep going or stop.

All Are Precious

So Jesus told them this story: "If a man has a hundred sheep and one of them gets lost, what will he do? Won't he leave the ninety-nine others in the wilderness and go to search for the one that is lost until he finds it? And when he has found it, he will joyfully carry it home on his shoulders. When he arrives, he will call together his friends and neighbors, saying, 'Rejoice with me because I have found my lost sheep.' In the same way, there is more joy in heaven over one lost sinner who repents and returns to God than over ninety-nine others who are righteous and haven't strayed away!"

Luke 15:3–7 NLT (also found in Matt. 18:12–14)

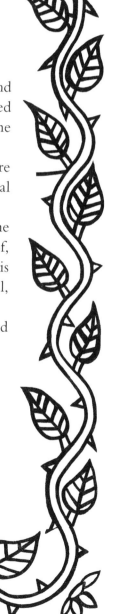

The nature of the gospel of Jesus can be so countercultural that it's easy to miss its meaning, beauty, and depth. For instance, in the parable of the lost sheep, Jesus compares himself to a shepherd with one hundred sheep. When one of those sheep is lost, the shepherd goes after it, leaving the remaining ninety-nine in the wilderness. Why? Because, to Jesus, one sheep is just as precious as ninety-nine.

But to our human mind-sets, if we have one hundred of anything—dollars, pieces of jewelry, friends—we're inclined to overlook the loss of one. After all, we still have ninety-nine dollars, lots of earrings, and plenty of gal pals to journey with.

Thankfully, Jesus doesn't see the one hundred the way we do. Each of us is just as valuable to him as all of the others. And like the shepherd who sought the lost sheep, Jesus desires to see all of us in the fold, taken care of, and led by our own Great Shepherd. There's no "Why did you do that? Didn't I tell you not to go there?" Nor is there "What were you thinking?" When we're lost, Jesus simply wants to welcome us home to the loving, joyful, peaceful, abundant life he offers (see John 10:10).

If you have wandered too far away from Christ, remember the sheep. Call out to the Shepherd and he will find you. Rejoice! You've been found.

My God, my Shepherd, thank you for loving me so much that you want me safely in your fold. I am sorry I have strayed. I accept your joyous invitation to return home.

The Lost Money

Or what woman having ten silver coins, if she loses one of them, does not light a lamp, sweep the house, and search carefully until she finds it? When she has found it, she calls together her friends and neighbors, saying, "Rejoice with me, for I have found the coin that I had lost." Just so, I tell you, there is joy in the presence of the angels of God over one sinner who repents.

Luke 15:8–10 NRSV

Now, here's a relatable parable, hardly any interpretation needed. No sheep, nor servants, nor soil. A woman is searching for a missing coin. She has ten precious silver coins, each worth about one day's wage. It's the equivalent of a full day's wages being cut from a two-week paycheck. Ouch!

No way is this woman, who has probably worked very hard for her money, going to let it be lost without a full-on search. Can't you see her pulling out the lamp (she needs good light for this search) and looking underneath the chairs? She gets the broom out and sweeps her house thoroughly. It's imperative to find this coin. No, she's not forgetting the nine others she has, but the lost one is just as valuable and necessary as the others. One day's wage cannot be forsaken. Oh, how her heart must soar when she spots the lone silver coin. Lost but now found. Missing but now reunited with the others.

Likewise, our heavenly Father rejoices when we turn from our sins and accept his gift of salvation. Each and every time one of us returns to where we belong, God rejoices. She once was lost, but now she's found. She was once blind, but now she sees.

Whom do you need to share this parable with today? God is waiting to rejoice yet another time.

Write a letter to a friend who may need to be reminded that God awaits his or her return to the fold. Consider giving her today's devotion and coloring page.

A Celebration

The father said to him, "Son, you are always with me, and all that I have is yours. We had to celebrate and be happy because your brother was dead, but now he is alive. He was lost, but now he is found."
Luke 15:31–32 NCV (full parable found in Luke 15:11–32)

You probably recall Jesus' provocative parable of a man asking for his inheritance before his father even dies, often called the Prodigal Son. This man wants to experience the pleasure of having fun now. He wants to spend his fortune—well, his portion of his father's fortune—now. Why wait until his father has died to enjoy the spoils and experiences that can be bought with his inheritance? It's somewhat understandable if you can get past the entitlement this young man clearly felt.

The father doesn't try to convince his son to stay and wait until the appointed time to receive his inheritance; he grants his son's wish. This cannot end well—or can it? The son enjoys himself in a manner akin to winning the lottery. He can buy whatever his heart desires. But ask those who've gotten rich quickly: the money rarely lasts. And even worse, the people who show up during the high times are rarely available in the low times.

The son realizes he has been foolish right around the time he wants to eat the same meal as the dirty pigs, but he can't even get a pod (v. 16). So he ventures home to ask his father for a servant's position (v. 19). Hard times have taught him humility.

Before he makes it all the way home, the young man sees his father running toward him. He is given a robe, a ring, sandals, and the assurance that he is still a son. The overjoyed father throws a celebration. The child who was lost has now returned.

The other son suffers his father's reaction. He has been faithful, never strayed, and worked to earn his inheritance. Ironically, he, too, suffers from an entitled attitude. Everything these sons have or will have belongs first to the father. They should just be happy to be a part of the family.

In life we may find ourselves as the prodigal, lost to selfish desire, or the brother who resents following the rules without receiving extra benefits. But we can still find joy in our Father's love. He loves all of his children and rejoices when they come to understand his truth. He rejoices as much when they faithfully stay near to him. Today, whichever son you identify with more, know that God is happy to have you in the family—always!

Dear God, I thank you for making me a part of your family. You are a gracious and loving parent. I receive and accept your bountiful love this day.

Be Wise Stewards

The manager thought to himself, "Now what? My boss has fired me. I don't have the strength to dig ditches, and I'm too proud to beg. Ah, I know how to ensure that I'll have plenty of friends who will give me a home when I am fired."

So he invited each person who owed money to his employer to come and discuss the situation. He asked the first one, "How much do you owe him?" The man replied, "I owe him 800 gallons of olive oil." So the manager told him, "Take the bill and quickly change it to 400 gallons."

The rich man had to admire the dishonest rascal for being so shrewd. And it is true that the children of this world are more shrewd in dealing with the world around them than are the children of the light. Here's the lesson: Use your worldly resources to benefit others and make friends. Then, when your earthly possessions are gone, they will welcome you to an eternal home.

If you are faithful in little things, you will be faithful in large ones. But if you are dishonest in little things, you won't be honest with greater responsibilities.

Luke 16:3–6, 8–10 NLT (full parable can be found in Luke 16:1–13)

Today's parable is Jesus' story of a manager who was about to get fired because he had been mishandling money. The man's rich boss had already let him know that he was not pleased with his work. So the manager, knowing that he will be without a job, makes a deal with the people who owe his rich boss. The manager cuts their debt, thereby making friends with those in debt to his boss. Surely they will remember the manager's kindness and help him out in his time of need.

When the rich man finds out what the manager says, he exclaims: "*Now* you decide to be smart and handle business!"

Yes, the rich man admired how the manager went about securing his future and collecting some of the debt. Why couldn't the manager do this when his job wasn't in jeopardy? After all, that's what he was paid to do: collect and manage his boss's money.

Now, Jesus isn't sharing this story to glorify the manager's business tactics or even his work ethic. The point is that we should be wise and shrewd. That makes sense. But we should be wise and shrewd because we recognize the eternal benefit. We're not getting money or resources just to accumulate them. We should be using them to build God's Kingdom and share his message with others. And yes, we should be wise with our resources—after all, we need to be trusted with the things of the earth in order to be trusted with eternal, more beneficial things.

Be wise. Be shrewd. And always remember you're really working for God, the richest boss around.

God, my Boss and Leader, give me the wisdom and discernment to handle all resources well. Help me to handle my time, my finances, and my gifts in a manner that honors you and brings others closer to you. I desire to be faithful over small things so you can trust me with greater things.

Before It's Too Late

There was a rich man who was clothed in purple and fine linen and who feasted sumptuously every day. And at his gate was laid a poor man named Lazarus, covered with sores, who desired to be fed with what fell from the rich man's table. Moreover, even the dogs came and licked his sores. The poor man died and was carried by the angels to Abraham's side. The rich man also died and was buried, and in Hades, being in torment, he lifted up his eyes and saw Abraham far off and Lazarus at his side. And he called out, "Father Abraham, have mercy on me, and send Lazarus to dip the end of his finger in water and cool my tongue, for I am in anguish in this flame." But Abraham said, "Child, remember that you in your lifetime received your good things, and Lazarus in like manner bad things; but now he is comforted here, and you are in anguish. And besides all this, between us and you a great chasm has been fixed, in order that those who would pass from here to you may not be able, and none may cross from there to us." And he said, "Then I beg you, father, to send him to my father's house—for I have five brothers—so that he may warn them, lest they also come into this place of torment." But Abraham said, "They have Moses and the Prophets; let them hear them." And he said, "No, father Abraham, but if someone goes to them from the dead, they will repent." He said to him, "If they do not hear Moses and the Prophets, neither will they be convinced if someone should rise from the dead."

Luke 16:19–31 ESV

The story of Lazarus and the rich man in this parable can be a tough pill to swallow, but the wise will take heed and apply its truths. It's a warning against being hardheaded, ungenerous, and unrepentant—conditions we all suffer at times.

Lazarus, the poor man who often sat at the gate of the rich man's home, just wished to eat the crumbs from the rich man's table. However, there's no evidence that the rich man was compassionate or generous to Lazarus.

Even in anguish, even in his despair, having died and been sent to Hades, the rich man still saw Lazarus as nothing but a servant. But Lazarus, who interestingly is the only person given a name in all of the parables, was rewarded and given a seat next to Father Abraham. God doesn't see people as we see people!

Thinking about hell and the consequences of sin isn't comforting or fun, but we should consider the cost of our actions while we still have a chance to repent. Are you overlooking the least of these to satisfy your own selfish needs? Have you listened to Scripture and applied it to your life? Have you accepted Christ's free gift of salvation and picked up your cross to truly follow him? Is the comfort of this life blocking you from grasping the true reward of eternal life? Whom do you need to share the gospel with before it is too late?

What Is Fair?

At the end of the day, the owner of the field said to the boss of all the workers, "Call the workers and pay them all. Start by paying the last people I hired. Then pay all of them, ending with the ones I hired first."

The workers who were hired at five o'clock came to get their pay. Each worker got one silver coin. Then the workers who were hired first came to get their pay. They thought they would be paid more than the others. But each one of them also received one silver coin. When they got their silver coin, they complained to the man who owned the land. They said, "Those people were hired last and worked only one hour. But you paid them the same as us. And we worked hard all day in the hot sun."

But the man who owned the field said to one of them, "Friend, I am being fair with you. You agreed to work for one silver coin. Right? So take your pay and go. I want to give the man who was hired last the same pay I gave you. I can do what I want with my own money. Why would you be jealous because I am generous?"

So those who are last now will be first in the future. And those who are first now will be last in the future.

Matt. 20:8–16 ERV (full parable can be found in Matt. 20:1–16)

The issue of fairness can be big for those of us who think we are living a righteous and holy life. Why do we sacrifice and try to live right while others seem to do whatever they want without concern? It can be frustrating. But Jesus, whose parables address the struggles of being Christian, had a story for this one, too.

A landowner paid some people to work for him. He told them how much he would pay them, they agreed, and they got to work. Now, he gave the same deal to everyone, no matter what time they started working. He first paid one silver coin to those who started later in the day. Then he continued distributing one silver coin each to the workers, from those who began second to last, to those who began working before all of the others. And when the first workers, the ones who had worked the longest, received one silver coin each, they were outraged. *How dare you give us the same amount you gave them? They only did a little work, but we've been out here working hard all day. What's wrong with you? Why are you treating your faithful workers like this?*

I can't say I wouldn't have joined in with this crowd; their complaint seems valid until Jesus presents the lesson. The landowner paid each worker the rate they agreed to before they began, exactly how much he said he would for the amount of work they did. Cut and dried.

When we sign up for this Christian journey, we should know what to expect and what's expected of us. We agree to the terms, so we shouldn't compare our journey to our neighbor's. We accept eternal, abundant life, and that's what we get. Now, if others receive the same for a different amount of time of service, that's between them and God. It's their agreement.

We'll do well to stop focusing on others and thank God for our covenantal agreement. It's the rate we were quoted, nothing less!

———

Gracious God, thank you for the gift of salvation. Thank you for giving me life, and life more abundant. I accept the terms of our agreement and will joyfully continue on this journey, sharing your Word and doing your will. Remind me to focus on our relationship, not on what I see around me. I want to keep my mind fixed on you so I can remain in perfect peace.

Keep Persisting

Now Jesus was telling the disciples a parable to make the point that at all times they ought to pray and not give up and lose heart, saying, "In a certain city there was a judge who did not fear God and had no respect for man. There was a [desperate] widow in that city and she kept coming to him and saying, 'Give me justice and legal protection from my adversary.' For a time he would not; but later he said to himself, 'Even though I do not fear God nor respect man, yet because this widow continues to bother me, I will give her justice and legal protection; otherwise by continually coming she [will be an intolerable annoyance and she] will wear me out.'" Then the Lord said, "Listen to what the unjust judge says! And will not [our just] God defend and avenge His elect [His chosen ones] who cry out to Him day and night? Will He delay [in providing justice] on their behalf? I tell you that He will defend and avenge them quickly. However, when the Son of Man comes, will He find [this kind of persistent] faith on the earth?"

Luke 18:1–8 AMP

Persistence pays off, it's true. To remind us to pray persistently, constantly, to God, Jesus told the parable of an ungodly judge. This judge didn't fear God and he didn't respect man. He was not a good judge. But because the widow was resolute and would not give up seeking justice, he gave the poor woman what she sought.

If this judge could grant the woman what she wanted, how much more will God, our just Lord and Creator, give us if we are persistent? Those of us who are in a relationship with God through Christ should know that we have God as our judge, and he is ready to defend and avenge us. We have only to ask and believe.

Jesus ends the parable with a startling question we should all take to heart. While God is our faithful judge and provider, are we faithful to God? Can our faith be relied upon? Will God find us trusting, believing, and waiting when Jesus returns? We should not give up nor lose heart, no matter how things seem.

How strong is your faith? Pray and seek God for all things—even for more faith if you need it.

Humility

Then Jesus told this story to some who had great confidence in their own righteousness and scorned everyone else: "Two men went to the Temple to pray. One was a Pharisee, and the other was a despised tax collector. The Pharisee stood by himself and prayed this prayer: 'I thank you, God, that I am not a sinner like everyone else—cheaters, sinners, adulterers. I'm certainly not like that tax collector! I fast twice a week, and I give you a tenth of my income.'

"But the tax collector stood at a distance and dared not even lift his eyes to heaven as he prayed. Instead, he beat his chest in sorrow, saying, 'O God, be merciful to me, for I am a sinner.' I tell you, this sinner, not the Pharisee, returned home justified before God. For those who exalt themselves will be humbled, and those who humble themselves will be exalted."

Luke 18:9–14 NLT

Funny thing about being Christian: we can sometimes get cocky. It is weird how following God's laws, commandments, and direction can make us think that we are really righteous, when in actuality we shouldn't be praising ourselves, but God.

In the parable of the Pharisee and the tax collector, Jesus offers us clarity.

Although he was no religious leader like the Pharisee, God acknowledged the prayer of the tax collector, the one considered a sinner, and justified him.

It's not what we do (or don't do), as the Pharisee was keen to rattle off; it's our humility before God's amazing mercy and grace that puts us in the right relationship with God. Surely, if we could collect points toward salvation by our good actions, we'd have no need for a savior. But the wise know we all need mercy and are humbled by Christ's sacrifice.

We are made righteous through Christ and Christ alone.

O, Holy One, I recognize your amazing gift of grace and love for me. I thank you for having mercy on a sinner like me. I'm thankful for your sacrifice so I can live in your Kingdom. Keep me ever mindful of your gift. Amen.

Good Stewardship

While he had their attention, and because they were getting close to Jerusalem by this time and expectation was building that God's kingdom would appear any minute, he told this story:

"There was once a man descended from a royal house who needed to make a long trip back to headquarters to get authorization for his rule and then return. But first he called ten servants together, gave them each a sum of money, and instructed them, 'Operate with this until I return.' [. . .]

"The first said, 'Master, I doubled your money.'

"He said, 'Good servant! Great work! Because you've been trustworthy in this small job, I'm making you governor of ten towns.'

"The second said, 'Master, I made a fifty percent profit on your money.'

"He said, 'I'm putting you in charge of five towns.'

"The next servant said, 'Master, here's your money safe and sound. I kept it hidden in the cellar. To tell you the truth, I was a little afraid. I know you have high standards and hate sloppiness, and don't suffer fools gladly.'

"He said, 'You're right that I don't suffer fools gladly—and you've acted the fool! Why didn't you at least invest the money in securities so I would have gotten a little interest on it?'

"Then he said to those standing there, 'Take the money from him and give it to the servant who doubled my stake.' [. . .]

"He said, 'That's what I mean: Risk your life and get more than you ever dreamed of. Play it safe and end up holding the bag."

Luke 19:11–13, 16–24, 26 MSG (full parable can be found in Luke 19:11–26)

Jesus wanted his followers to know how to live, even as they awaited the coming of the Kingdom. He didn't—and still doesn't—want people to sit around idly waiting until all is made right. We as Christians have some work to do—now.

God doesn't expect us to all do the same amount of work, but he does want us all to do the best we can with what we've been given.

Our lives are comparable to those in the parable. We've been given something from God—some of us a lot, some of us seemingly less. We shouldn't bury our gifts or talents or resources; instead we should make good investments, get some return on what God has given us, use our gifts, and produce more. We don't want to miss out on the joy of living as part of God's Kingdom, or have our gifts taken away from us because we refused to use them. Use your life and all you have been given to glorify the Lord.

How are you using your God-given gifts? How do you think God rates your return on investment? What can you do to make more use of your talents?

Good Intentions

"What do you think? A man had two sons. And he went to the first and said, 'Son, go and work in the vineyard today.' And he answered, 'I will not,' but afterward he changed his mind and went. And he went to the other son and said the same. And he answered, 'I go, sir,' but did not go. Which of the two did the will of his father?" They said, "The first." Jesus said to them, "Truly, I say to you, the tax collectors and the prostitutes go into the kingdom of God before you. For John came to you in the way of righteousness, and you did not believe him, but the tax collectors and the prostitutes believed him. And even when you saw it, you did not afterward change your minds and believe him."

Matt. 21:28–32 ESV

Good intentions really don't add up to much—unless, of course, they are followed by good actions. And Jesus brought home that point in his parable about workers in a vineyard. He said that a man asked for help from his two sons. The first one said he wouldn't work in the vineyard, but later he changed his mind and went ahead and helped his father out. Now the other son said he'd go, but he never really got around to it. So Jesus, in his amazing teaching style, asked his followers, "Which of the two did the will of his father?"

It's not a trick question. It's pretty simple. The one who actually did the work did the will of his father. It really didn't matter that the first son initially said no or that the second son agreed to help. What really mattered was what happened—their actions.

The same holds true for us today. It doesn't matter if you know the Bible, quote the Bible, and say you're a Christian if your actions don't line up. You may intend to do well, but actions can betray your best intentions. Yet, while many others may not say the right words or quote Scripture, they do God's will. They live godly lives through their actions.

Let's not get caught up in what we say, but let's follow through on our good words and intentions and actually do the will of God.

What are your actions saying? Are your actions in line with your intentions? How can you bring your words and actions closer into alignment with God's will today?

Give Respect

Jesus then began to speak to them in parables: "A man planted a vineyard. He put a wall around it, dug a pit for the winepress and built a watchtower. Then he rented the vineyard to some farmers and moved to another place. At harvest time he sent a servant to the tenants to collect from them some of the fruit of the vineyard. But they seized him, beat him and sent him away empty-handed. Then he sent another servant to them; they struck this man on the head and treated him shamefully. He sent still another, and that one they killed. He sent many others; some of them they beat, others they killed.

"He had one left to send, a son, whom he loved. He sent him last of all, saying, 'They will respect my son.'

"But the tenants said to one another, 'This is the heir. Come, let's kill him, and the inheritance will be ours.' So they took him and killed him, and threw him out of the vineyard.

"What then will the owner of the vineyard do? He will come and kill those tenants and give the vineyard to others. Haven't you read this passage of Scripture:

"'The stone the builders rejected
has become the cornerstone;
the Lord has done this,
and it is marvelous in our eyes'?"

Mark 12:1–11 NIV (also found in Matt. 21:33–45 and Luke 20:9–19)

Along with teaching about the new Way he was sharing, Jesus also didn't leave his followers blind about what was going to happen to him. Jesus knew that he would be crucified for our sins. He knew that he would be led to death (and resurrected) as a part of his mission to rescue us, and he revealed this through parables.

In this parable, God is compared to a landowner or landlord who rents his vineyard to tenants. When the landowner sends his servants to collect some of the harvest from the tenants, the tenants are noncompliant. They don't want to pay up, so they mistreat the servants. Then the landowner sends his own son to collect the debts, and they kill him, which prompts the landowner to return in person and deal directly with the evil tenants. He takes his land from the noncompliant tenants and gives his land to others, tenants who cherish the opportunity they have been given and joyfully return their harvest to the landowner.

When Jesus first told this story, it was directed at the people of God who didn't listen to the prophets sent to tell them to repent and turn to the Lord completely. Those same people killed God's Son when he was sent to earth. But God's plans were still carried out. The very one who was rejected became the center of the Christian faith—the ultimate sacrifice for sin.

Now, as the recipients of this great gift, we have a choice: bear fruit for our landlord (God) or refuse to bear fruit in keeping with all we have been given through Christ. Either way it goes, God will not be mocked. God's plans will go forth. Don't be a tenant who lives on the land but doesn't return the fruit to the owner or listen to his prophets or Son. We who have accepted Christ can reap the benefits of salvation and bear fruit reflective of our landlord (God). We can embrace the gift of Christ and return the praise and honor to God through our lifestyle (the fruit we bear).

Write a thank-you note to God for the gift of salvation today.

The Invitation

When the king entered and looked over the scene, he spotted a man who wasn't properly dressed. He said to him, "Friend, how dare you come in here looking like that!" The man was speechless. Then the king told his servants, "Get him out of here—fast. Tie him up and ship him to hell. And make sure he doesn't get back in."

That's what I mean when I say, "Many get invited; only a few make it."

Matt. 22:11–14 MSG (full parable found in Matt. 22:2–14; also found in Luke 14:16–24)

Sometimes it seems like the Christian lifestyle is too hard. It's work to follow all the rules of living according to God's Word. But consider Jesus' parable. On the surface it seems harsh, but it actually shows us just how much God cares for us.

Jesus says that a man had a feast, a big celebration for his son's wedding. This man spared no expense and offered the choicest food and drink to the guests. The man sent his servants out to find the guests and let them know that the party had started, that those invited should come and enjoy themselves.

But for some reason, the invited guests had a lot of excuses as to why they couldn't attend the banquet. Some even beat up the messengers. They apparently really didn't want to attend this party!

So the man throwing the party told his servants: "Go out and find anyone off the street. Tell them it's free food and a good party." Not only did the man invite the homeless to the party, but he also apparently gave them some fine clothes to wear, too. It was a custom to send the appropriate attire with the invitation. All right, now that sounds like a party.

But one guest apparently showed up without the gifted clothing. He was thrown out of the party and sent to his death. The man throwing the party was furious. It was as if the guest wanted to come and eat the goodies but not wear the proper clothes—which were already provided for him.

Whoa. Are we like that guest? Do we want the benefits of salvation—the nice meal and the awesome party— but we don't want to put on the attire that's already been given to us? Are we opening ourselves up daily to God's Spirit, the true garment of praise, or are we trying to nibble off the banquet table without getting dressed properly?

Even still, have we decided not to attend this party although we have been graciously invited and the limo and dress are awaiting us? What excuses could we possibly have not to attend?

Throw away your excuses and join the party. God's made a way for you to live holy—accept the clothing of God's Spirit and enjoy the goodness of the banquet. It's not hard. It just takes a made-up mind and heart. The party host wants you here. Don't snub God. Accept your invitation. Have you RSVP'd for this party yet?

Write a letter to the host, God, accepting the invitation. Thank God for your attire that is already provided and available through the Spirit.

Pay Attention

Now learn a lesson from the fig tree. When its branches bud and its leaves begin to sprout, you know that summer is near. In the same way, when you see all these things taking place, you can know that his return is very near, right at the door. I tell you the truth, this generation will not pass from the scene before all these things take place. Heaven and earth will disappear, but my words will never disappear.

However, no one knows the day or hour when these things will happen, not even the angels in heaven or the Son himself. Only the Father knows. And since you don't know when that time will come, be on guard! Stay alert!

Mark 13:28–33 NLT (also found in Matt. 24:32–44 and Luke 21:29–33)

God's timetable is so amazing. We can even be reminded of God's plans just by paying attention to nature. Seasons change, but not without warning. We see the branches begin to bud and leaves sprout between spring and summer, signifying a change. We feel cooler nights and see trees change colors at the start of autumn. And when branches are bare and days are colder, we know winter is upon us. And in this parable, Jesus wants us to know that just as we see the seasons change, we will have some warning of when the end will be near. We have signs. We will have signals reminding us of God's promise to send Jesus again to reign forever.

But, lest we get careless and lazy, assuming we will know the exact day, remember that we do not know the day nor the hour when he will return. Angels don't even know the day, nor does Jesus. Only God knows.

Therefore, since this date is a mystery, we should always be ready. We should stay on guard and be alert.

We can rejoice and hope in God's faithfulness, even as we see the seasons change. We can trust and believe that the great day will come when we can live in peace in God's Kingdom, but we don't know when it will be. So live each day as if it were the last. Love. Laugh. Share. Pray. Wait. Hope. Rejoice. Give.

What will you do today to live in anticipation of Jesus' coming?

Faithful or Not?

Who then is the faithful, thoughtful, and *wise servant, whom his master has put in charge of his household to give to the others the food* and *supplies at the proper time?*

Blessed (happy, fortunate, and to be envied) is that servant whom, when his master comes, he will find so doing.

I solemnly declare to you, he will set him over all his possessions.

But if that servant is wicked and says to himself, My master is delayed and *is going to be gone a long time,*

And begins to beat his fellow servants and to eat and drink with the drunken,

The master of that servant will come on a day when he does not expect him and at an hour of which he is not aware,

And will punish him [cut him up by scourging] and put him with the pretenders (hypocrites); there will be weeping and grinding of teeth.

Matt. 24:45–51 AMPC

Which servant will you be like when our Lord returns? The one who is faithfully and wisely tending to those put in your care, shining your light, and living as your Master expects? Or the wicked servant who looks at the calendar and doesn't expect the Lord's return to be any time soon, so you live life on your own terms, forgoing the instructions from your Master?

Use this parable as a strong warning. You don't want to be caught with your work undone, foolishly expecting our Lord's return to be far away. Do what you know you should be doing—today. Live as if you expect Christ to return now.

What will you do differently today in anticipation of Christ's return?

The Wedding Day

God's kingdom is like ten young virgins who took oil lamps and went out to greet the bridegroom. Five were silly and five were smart. The silly virgins took lamps, but no extra oil. The smart virgins took jars of oil to feed their lamps. The bridegroom didn't show up when they expected him, and they all fell asleep.

In the middle of the night someone yelled out, "He's here! The bridegroom's here! Go out and greet him!"

The ten virgins got up and got their lamps ready. The silly virgins said to the smart ones, "Our lamps are going out; lend us some of your oil."

They answered, "There might not be enough to go around; go buy your own."

They did, but while they were out buying oil, the bridegroom arrived. When everyone who was there to greet him had gone into the wedding feast, the door was locked.

Much later, the other virgins, the silly ones, showed up and knocked on the door, saying, "Master, we're here. Let us in."

He answered, "Do I know you? I don't think I know you."

So stay alert. You have no idea when he might arrive.

Matt. 25:1–13 MSG

Can you imagine knowing exactly what you need to do to reach your ultimate goal in life, having all the tools ready, having heard and understood the orders and commands, and even having the desire to get there...but you don't? That's exactly how the five silly virgins in today's parable must have felt.

They, along with the five smart virgins, knew the bridegroom was coming. I think all ten of the virgins in this story had faith and believed that they would meet up with the bridegroom and live happily ever after. But the silly ones did something, well, rather silly. They packed too little oil. They didn't bring any extra. They figured they had enough. They were wrong, and they missed out.

Oh, if they could tell their tale. Oh, if they could redo their situation. The silly virgins had some oil. They had some faith and hope that the bridegroom would return for them...but they weren't fully prepared. They missed the day. They missed the mark. All because they weren't truly ready.

I don't want to be like those five silly virgins, eager to get the prize but, oops, unprepared. I need more oil. I know you don't want to be like that, either. Stay alert. Be ready. Keep praying and watching and waiting and hoping. Our bridegroom is coming. Always be prepared.

What are you doing to stay ready for the coming of Christ? Do you have enough oil packed?

Be on Guard

Be on guard and stay constantly alert [and pray]; for you do not know when the appointed *time will come. It is like a man away on a journey,* who *when he left home put his servants in charge, each with his* particular *task, and also ordered the doorkeeper to be* continually *alert. Therefore, be* continually *on the alert—for you do not know when the master of the house is coming, whether in the evening, or at midnight, or when the rooster crows, or in the morning—[stay alert,] in case he should come suddenly* and *unexpectedly* and *find you asleep* and *unprepared. What I say to you I say to everyone, "Be on the alert [stay awake and be continually cautious]!"*

Mark 13:33–37 AMP

How do we wait? How do we stay prepared? What do we do while we wait on God, on Jesus' second coming, and on all the other promises God has given to us?

This parable gives us some guidance. We should always be ready, expecting today to be the day. We should always be alert, expecting God to deliver right now. Staying in constant prayer will keep us focused on God and all that he has promised to bring.

No, we do not know when anything will really happen. But we can be confident that it will. So, we wait with anticipation. We wait with hope. We wait prepared to receive the promise now, and tomorrow, and the next day. We bring all we need to be prepared: our prayers, our work, our reminders, and our oil.

We look at the signs, aware that they cannot be fully interpreted by us but that they can remind us of God's faithfulness. We listen for the rooster to crow. We look at the changing of seasons. We greet the morning and bid farewell to the night.

Living in the in-between can be hard, but we mustn't give up. We've been called to be alert and ready. We each have a task. Be on guard. Show up prepared until the end. Our reward is great and worth the wait.

Heavenly Lord, give me all I need to stay prepared and on guard as I await your arrival. I trust and believe your Word and I hope in the plans you've prepared for me through Christ. I don't want to run this race in vain, so help me to endure and persevere to receive my reward. Amen.

No Excuses

The servant given one thousand said, "Master, I know you have high standards and hate careless ways, that you demand the best and make no allowances for error. I was afraid I might disappoint you, so I found a good hiding place and secured your money. Here it is, safe and sound down to the last cent."

The master was furious. "That's a terrible way to live! It's criminal to live cautiously like that! If you knew I was after the best, why did you do less than the least? The least you could have done would have been to invest the sum with the bankers, where at least I would have gotten a little interest.

"Take the thousand and give it to the one who risked the most. And get rid of this 'play-it-safe' who won't go out on a limb. Throw him out into utter darkness."

Matt. 25:24–30 MSG (full parable found in Matt. 25:14–30)

A few parables are found in several gospels, showing that several writers picked up on the same lessons Jesus shared. However, the parable of the talents is written and titled differently in Luke and Matthew. This story picks up with a concept similar to the parable of the minas. A master, in this story, returns to see how his servants have done with his money. He, like the king in the book of Luke, wanted to get a return on his investments. He wanted his servants to make the best use of the money (or gifts) he had entrusted to each of them.

When the first one says he made a profit, the master is pleased and makes the servant a partner. When the next one says the same thing, the master makes him a partner also. Giving God our best and making use of all he's given us—whether it is money, talent, or other resources—makes us partners with God, co-creators in bringing about the Kingdom of God. What an honor. What a privilege. What joyful news.

But there's also a sobering message in this story. When the master visits the servant who did not get a return on his investment, there is a severe price to pay. The servant lets the master know his reasons for not doing anything with his talent—he gives his master excuses, pure and simple. No matter the reason for not doing our best and getting a return on God's investment in us, it's just that: an excuse.

We should be willing and enthusiastic participants in God's work. God has gifted each of us with one or more special gifts, talents, resources, and so on. It's up to us to do our best and use them for good, getting the best return on God's investment. Don't be left handing God an excuse when he shows up and asks for an account of the investment he made in you.

What's holding you back from giving your best and using your God-given talents? Make a plan to wipe out the excuses.

Sheep or Goat?

But when the Son of Man comes in his glory, and all the angels with him, then he will sit upon his glorious throne. All the nations will be gathered in his presence, and he will separate the people as a shepherd separates the sheep from the goats. He will place the sheep at his right hand and the goats at his left.

Then the King will say to those on his right, "Come, you who are blessed by my Father, inherit the Kingdom prepared for you from the creation of the world. For I was hungry, and you fed me. I was thirsty, and you gave me a drink. I was a stranger, and you invited me into your home. I was naked, and you gave me clothing. I was sick, and you cared for me. I was in prison, and you visited me."

Then these righteous ones will reply, "Lord, when did we ever see you hungry and feed you? Or thirsty and give you something to drink? Or a stranger and show you hospitality? Or naked and give you clothing? When did we ever see you sick or in prison and visit you?"

And the King will say, "I tell you the truth, when you did it to one of the least of these my brothers and sisters, you were doing it to me!"

Matt. 25:31–40 NLT (full parable found in Matt. 25:31–46)

It's what we live for—the glorious coming of our King, the opening up of a new world where there is no sickness, death, pain, or sorrow (see Rev. 21:4). It's promised to all who believe, and we wait in anticipation of that marvelous and eternal celebration.

Will you be on the side with the other sheep, separated from the goats, placed at the right hand of Christ? There's a simple way to find out. Review your life. Check out your actions. Do they line up with the deeds told in this story? Have you fed the hungry and given drink to the thirsty? Have you shown the stranger unbiased hospitality and provided clothes for those without? Have you visited the sick and incarcerated?

That's exactly what the sheep did. And it was as if they were doing these deeds for God. Ah, to be a servant of God, ever reflecting his nature throughout my day and through my actions. That is my prayer.

Holy One, I can't wait to live eternally with you. Make me ever ready. Show me who is in need. Show me how to care. Remind me that I'm showing you love when I care for your people. I desire to please you. I am a sheep, looking to follow my Shepherd. Amen.